Polar Bear vs. Seal

Revised Edition

Mary Meinking

Raintree
Chicago Illinois

www.capstonepub.com
Visit our website to find out more information about Heinemann-Raintree books.

To order:
☎ Phone 800-747-4992
🖳 Visit www.capstonepub.com
   to browse our catalog and order online.

Edited by Rebecca Rissman, Dan Nunn,
    and Catherine Veitch
Designed by Joanna Hinton Malivoire
Levelling by Jeanne Clidas
Picture research by Hannah Taylor
Production by Victoria Fitzgerald
Originated by Capstone Global Library

Library of Congress Cataloging-in-Publication Data
Meinking, Mary.
  Polar bear vs. seal / Mary Meinking.
    p. cm. —— (Predator vs. prey)
  Includes bibliographical references and index.
  ISBN 978-1-4109-9813-2 (paperback)
  ISBN 978-1-4109-9814-9 (ebook)
1. Polar bear—Food—Juvenile literature. 2. Seals (Animals)—Defenses—Juvenile literature. 3. Predation (Biology)—Juvenile literature. I. Title.
  QL737.C27M45 2011
  599.786'153—dc22

Acknowledgments
We would like to thank the following for permission to reproduce photographs: Alamy: Radius Images, 20, RGB Ventures/SuperStock, cover top, 25, Steven J. Kazlowski, 8, 15, 16; BluePlanetArchive.com: Bryan & Cherry Alexander, 4; FLPA: Imagebroker, 18, Minden Pictures/Flip Nicklin, 11, Minden Pictures/Tui De Roy, cover bottom, 7, Sunset, 21; Getty Images: KAZUHIRO NOGI, 24, Paul Souders, 5, 9; iStockphoto: Visual Communications, 6; Nature Picture Library: Andy Rouse, 17, Mats Forsberg, 22, Steven Kazlowski, 12; Newscom: Courtesy of Paul Nicklen, Supplied by PacificCoastNews, 10; Shutterstock: GTW, 29, jo Crebbin, 23, Ondrej Prosicky, 28, polarman, 19, Sandra Ophorst, 26, Vlad G, 27; SuperStock: NHPA, 13, Steven Kazlowski, 14

We would like to thank Michael Bright for his invaluable help in the preparation of this book.

Every effort has been made to contact copyright holders of any material reproduced in this book. Any omissions will be rectified in subsequent printings if notice is given to the publisher.

All the Internet addresses (URLs) given in this book were valid at the time of going to press. However, due to the dynamic nature of the Internet, some addresses may have changed, or sites may have changed or ceased to exist since publication. While the author and publisher regret any inconvenience this may cause readers, no responsibility for any such changes can be accepted by either the author or the publisher.

Some words are shown in bold, **like this**. You can find out what they mean by looking in the glossary.

Contents

Icy Battle

Claws slash! Flippers splash! Two animals meet in an icy white battlefield. Here is the world's largest **carnivore** on land, the polar bear. It is up against a slippery challenger, the seal.

seal

The competitors live in the icy **Arctic**. Both have strengths that will help them in this battle.

PREDATOR
polar bear

LENGTH: 10 feet

WEIGHT: 1,400 pounds

SAME SIZE AS: a medium-sized car

Key
where polar bears and Arctic ringed seals live

PREY
Arctic ringed seal

LENGTH: 4 feet

WEIGHT: 115 pounds

SAME SIZE AS: a large dog

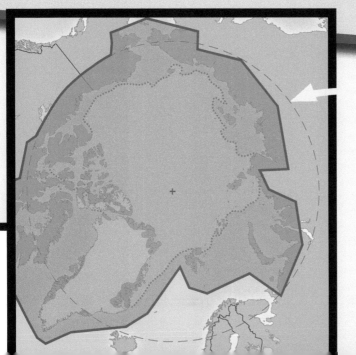

Arctic

King of the North

Polar bears live alone. They cross the ice and snow and swim in the sea looking for food. They wander over 40 miles every day. That's farther than 580 football fields.

Did You Know?

Polar bears can be found a long way from the shore. Sometimes they float on big chunks of ice, like rafts.

Hold Their Breath

The seal swims under the ice like a fish. But it's a **mammal**. So it comes up for air every 8 to 15 minutes.

Did You Know?

Seals use their front claws to make air holes in the ice so they can breathe. Some holes go through nearly seven feet of ice!

Who's Hungry?

The polar bear is a **carnivore**, or meat eater. It often eats seals. The polar bear lies next to seal air holes. It waits for a seal to come up for air. If one appears, the polar bear grabs it. But it can be a long wait.

air hole

Polar bears can go for six days without eating!

13

Sneak Attack

One morning the seal climbs onto the ice to lay in the sun. But it stays close to its air hole. The polar bear heads across the ice looking for **prey**. It sniffs the air. Soon it picks up a **scent,** or special smell.

Did You Know?
A polar bear can smell a seal from 1/2 a mile away. That's about 1,000 steps away!

The polar bear quietly slides into the icy water. Its long neck keeps its head out of the water when it swims. Then the polar bear crawls out onto the ice. It shakes itself off, like a dog.

Did You Know?
Polar bears are strong swimmers. They can swim up to 60 miles without stopping. That's farther than 75 city blocks!

The polar bear follows the **scent** until it spots the seal. The polar bear looks for the best place to sneak up on the seal. Seals cannot see things that are far away very well.

Did You Know?

The biggest danger for Arctic seals is not the polar bear—it's **global warming**! Much of their icy home is melting as the weather gets warmer.

The polar bear gets down low and creeps slowly toward the seal. It is hard for the seal to see and hear the bear. The polar bear's white coat **blends** in with the snow and ice.

Did You Know?

The polar bear has huge 12-inch-wide paws. These dinner plate-sized paws have fur on the bottom. This helps them sneak around quietly.

Did You Know?

Polar bears can run up to 25 miles per hour. That's twice as fast as the average adult running speed!

When the polar bear is close, it **charges** at the seal. The seal sees the bear coming. It uses its front flippers to drag itself over the ice. It wriggles toward the water. The polar bear gets closer and closer until the seal reaches the water's edge.

The seal dives in! It shoots down deep like a **torpedo**. Its front flippers steer and its rear flippers push it through the water like a fish. The polar bear dives into the sea after the seal, but it can't go as deep as the seal.

And the Winner Is...

...the seal! Seals are better swimmers than polar bears. They can hold their breath for up to 45 minutes and dive down to 300 feet. That's as deep as a 30-story building is tall!

Polar bears can only stay under water for two minutes.

What Are the Odds?

Polar bears catch **prey** once out of every 50 tries! They only catch a seal every four or five days. Polar bears need to eat lots of fat, or **blubber**, for energy. Seals have thick layers of blubber, which makes them great meals!

Glossary

Arctic area around the North Pole

blend when things look so alike that you cannot tell them apart

blubber thick layer of fat under animals' skin

carnivore animal that eats meat

charge rush or attack

global warming rise in temperature of the surface of the Earth, including the land, sea, and air. This causes weather changes around the world.

mammal warm-blooded animal that feeds its young milk

predator animal that hunts other animals

prey animal that is hunted by other animals for food

scent smell given off by an animal

torpedo explosive missile shot underwater at a target

Find Out More

Books

Ganeri, Anita. *Animal Top Tens: The Polar Regions' Most Amazing Animals.* Chicago: Raintree, 2008.

Rosing, Norbert. *Face to Face with Polar Bears.* Washington, DC: National Geographic Society, 2009.

Spilsbury, Louise. *Seal.* Chicago: Heinemann Library, 2010.

Websites

http://gowild.wwf.org.uk/gowild/amazing_animals/
On this Website you can find out more about polar bears and other amazing animals and watch videos of them in the wild.

http://kids.nationalgeographic.com/Animals/CreatureFeature/Polar-bear
Learn more about polar bears on this Website.

http://www.ecokids.ca/pub/eco_info/topics/field_guide/mammals/ringed_seal.cfm
Find out more about the Ringed seal on this Website.

Index